The Nature of God and Human Spiritual Evolution

THE NEW AWAKENING

JEFFREY THOMAS FAIRHURST

PAGE PUBLISHING
Conneaut Lake, PA

First originally published by
Page Publishing 2024

ISBN 979-8-89315-274-6 (pbk)
ISBN 979-8-89315-281-4 (digital)

Printed in the United States of America

This book is dedicated to all the unknown and forgotten soldiers who have stood up against evil tyranny over history. To those who have fought for freedom. To our teachers over time who have attempted to teach us how to become a more civilized species and have fed good food to our heads. To our children and grandchildren in hopes of a better day for posterity. To those who were kind to me along my journey through the valley of the poor while I attended the University of Hard Knocks.

CONTENTS

ACKNOWLEDGMENT

I have had too many people play a role in my life to try and single out even a couple. Most everyone whom I have come across, the good and bad, even if I don't remember you in my conscious mind, have given me food for my head. The good ones gave me the proper food and examples. The bad ones taught me what I shouldn't do. Some things I learned quickly; other things I had to learn the hard way like a lot of folks.

Though I want to acknowledge Mr. and Mrs. Stroyd, who were my nanny and my male mentor for my first five and most important years of a child's development. To me, they were my parents. Mr. Stroyd had been a squad leader of a mortar section during World War II, who was captured by Rommel in North Africa. Mrs. Stroyd had been a first sergeant during the war in London and survived the Nazi's bombing of London. They were good people who tried to teach me to do the proper things during early childhood development. They came over from England on a five-year work visa, and after my fifth birthday, they moved away. My response was rebellion, and I became a wild child. I also must acknowledge the folks who adopted me and paid for my needs, wants, and the love of your family.

INTRODUCTION

There are over nine thousand various religious cults around the globe today claiming to have the answers and only pathway to heaven, each using fabricated stories to appease the superstitious minds of people. Who's right? Who's wrong? Are they even close? Being a process analyst by profession, I was compelled by thoughts to analyze and evaluate creation, physical and spiritual, using the laws/directives of nature and the scales of process. If you want to find a crook, follow the money. If you want to find our God of creation, follow the processes of nature up through the scales of process and the order of magnitude. This book is intended for those who seek truth in the reality of life and the process of natural creation and evolution/change regardless of your background. I am trying to write what needs to be said, but not too long so more people might want to read it. Yet where I repeat something, it is because it is a critical point, not regurgitating. The most important part of this book is the Cornerstone and Foundation of Human Understanding. Common grounds of understanding. Personally, I have zero power, none, zilch, to change a thing. The power of truth does. I am not trying to save anyone's soul. I can't; that is up to the individual. What I can do to help, though, is use the power of truth and truths of reality to be the authority of what my analysis reveals. Just because I write something does not mean that I like what needs to be understood. Truth can be very painful, and that is not my intent. So if the truth hurts, don't take it personally. I am doing what I have been taught, trained, and what experience has given me. Actually, for a while now, I have been feeling like a doctor who has to tell their patient that they have stage four cancer with two months to live. Only our Creator knows the date and time of humanity's fate.

Humanity has technically evolved leaps and bounds over the last two thousand years, spiritually held back by evil energy and ignorance passed down through the generations. Who I am is irrelevant. What is relevant is the truth and realities of spiritual and human nature. It is not my intent to create another religion, only to seek the truth of reality and provide honest feedback for those who do not appear to be part delusional and half-daft in relation to things unseen. Yet they do a decent job of helping others. Plus, the majority are not as delusional or as daft as those who so obviously are stuck in a mental state of denial relating to the physical and biological reality of being a male or female (damaged souls).

I am writing this book for the next epic time period of humanity, the post reckoning! Too many misguided souls in this time period. The effects of the information age caused chaos and confusion, with too much information for people to process and with data overload for people and societies to adjust to the rapid changing of the times. Trying to stay up on technology is like a dog trying to catch its tale. The minds of the children don't have the life experiences or the mental capacity to process the information, generating fears and emotional stress and confusion, finger-fornicating their cell phones like a majority of the adults wanting to tickle their emotions.

Before the Information Age, it took data/information a long time to reach the masses and create any long-term effects. Human emotional reactions and motion were very slow to form. With the World Wide Web, mass emotional reactions can occur in seconds. Humanity is running out of control—too much, too fast. In the scales of process, computers are like people—garbage in, *garbage out*! And like the Bible, you shouldn't believe everything you read. Process is process, and I am doing some debugging for your time period. I will leave some copies of this small book in a few time capsules in a couple of places buried. It has been very painful to watch the moral deterioration of our species over my life cycle. I reviewed human history, realizing why people want to forget it when I was done. This included learning about our teachers, from Moses to Ron L. Hubbard. Confucius understood way back in 530 BC that religions separate, not unite, the people and cause major human conflicts.

In the eternal battle between good and evil and the natural scales of process, it is the tactic of divide and conquer. Confucianism had major support from various leaders in China until 1911. No, I don't want to create a religion but a fellowship of a more realistic understanding of creation and that of our Creator if humanity gets another chance to get it right. The Fellowship of Spiritual Infinity (FOSI). Not a physical movement but a mutual spiritual understanding. Not writing to be nice or mean, just the truth as can be understood in this time period of human evolution. Are our brains getting smaller?

Yes, I have asked God, our Creator, for guidance, and my prayers were answered with the truth of reality. I started off by asking God for a weapon to fight the evil energies, and God gave me a weapon called Satan's nemesis. The weapon? Truth—the only weapon that can defeat the unbeatable foe. Then I prayed for the right approach to review and communicate using the laws of nature and the scales of process and received the bedrock of human understanding. I am well aware of the opposition this book will generate. I know that they are afraid of the truth exposing their false doctrines and control of their sheeple, flocks, and income.

For those of us born in America with our Constitution and the Bill of Rights, we are some of the most fortunate people on the globe. Starting with the First Amendment, the right of freedom of the press and speech, with freedom of religion for starters, with separation between church and state (for safety). Followed by the Second, with the right to bear arms to protect the first and the other amendments to the Constitution. Freedom to teach the freedom of speech. Freedom to preach for the freedom of speech to speak the truth! That was the intent of the freedom of the press. We all owe a debt of gratitude to those who have come before us, who have fought, and who have died in service to our country.

Fortunately for humanity as a whole, using a rough order of magnitude, the two most popular ideologies only have about 10 percent each who have been programmed to believe in them. Which means the major majority of the global population doesn't buy into stories that a physical body would rise up from death, wander around for thirty days or so, and then take off to outer space. To our primitive pagan ancestors, outer space was their perceived heavens, and the Earth was flat, making promises that if you put your faith in primitive pagan Greco-Roman mythology and propaganda, all your transgressions will be forgiven. Human nature tries and passes the buck and takes the easy way out. There are no shortcuts to our Creator's domain.

Claiming that our Creator is a blood-thirsty, barbaric god who would send his only son to be brutally tortured and *nailed* to a cross as human sacrifice to our Creator. Shame, shame, shame on *you*. Followed by the return of Joshua in the end times, they will all rise up from the dead like zombies and ascend into the heavens and live happily ever after, even giving themselves the power to forgive other people's sins so they could collect personal data, at one point even charging people for their indulgences, which led to the creation of another religion called the Protestants. Started by a fellow named Martin Luther in 1517. Followed by many years of war and tears of a few million dead. The same year, Syria and Egypt were taken over by the Ottoman Empire, controlled by Islam at the cost of many lives.

To answer the question of what happened to the body of Jesus, it was the Romans who disposed of Jesus's body, so there would not be a grave site for his followers to make pilgrimage. Out of sight, out of mind. After all, they were the ones who were supposed to guard his tomb, according to their scripture. The same thing happened recently with Osama Bin Laden's body being dumped at sea. Then a little over three hundred years later, the Roman emperor, Constantine, saw the opportunity to take the helm of Christianity to unite his army. A few years later, there was an ongoing schism with the leaders of the East and West Christians on whether or not Jesus was a god or a teacher. Constantine called for a council to settle the issue in AD 325, with himself as the overseeing authority. It was settled by his edict alone that Jesus was called a god after that. Why? Because a teacher didn't have the powers of the other pagan gods. The same guy who, in the following year, murdered his wife and eldest son! That is the character of the person who ultimately was responsible for the pontification of Jesus; the person's word so many people put their faith and trust in.

Nor does the majority of the global population believe the promise that there are seventy-two virgins waiting in heaven for them if they kill those who are not part of their religious cult and are taught to hate others and suppress the rights of females. Using sex to get followers. At least Islam doesn't bless same-sex marriages. Though they do have more primitive ways of dealing with the issues.

Unfortunately for humanity as a whole, our technological advancements in weaponry give religious fanatic cults the abilities of mass destruction. This can be prevented, but that is the road humanity is on in this epic period of human history. Change comes with the winds blowing puppets on a string, which always leaves the door open for hope. The following are self-evident realities of life and that of our Creator. So with no further ado…

THE CORNERSTONE AND FOUNDATION OF HUMAN UNDERSTANDING

1. Did you have a choice of where on the earth you were born?
2. Did you have a choice of when you were born?
3. Did you have a choice of who your parents were or who else may have raised you?
4. Did you have a choice of what language you were taught to speak?

5. Did you have a choice of what school or teachers you had in early education?
6. Did you have a choice of which religious theology you were taught to believe in or not?
7. Did you have a choice in becoming a biological male or female?
8. Did you have a choice in the color of your hair, eyes, or skin?

The Truth?

No, no, you did not have a choice, and neither has any other person ever born into this natural physical world.

1. If we are, then our Creator is.
2. Our Creator is not a racist.
3. Our Creator is not religious.

4. Our Creator wants to be loved, not feared.
5. Our Creator wants humanity to evolve into a loving civilized species.

Do you fear the wrath of God? If so, then you have been mistakenly misled. Our Creator only wants to be loved by us, not feared. Love is God's nature. Fear is human nature. What each of us does need to fear are the bad decisions we make over the course of our individual physical life cycle. We all need to fear the unseen and unknown, like the things we have hidden away in our subconscious mind. The processes of nature are God's ways and means for creation and life to exist as we know it. Nature has four parts: one, physical visual matter; two, physical unseen matter (with the naked eye); three, invisible energy currents; and fourth, the spiritual energies.

For each part to exist, natural, multidimensional, behavioral boundaries of motion are in place to control the balance, stabilizing the environments with constraints for natural growth and expansion, which are defined by the laws of physical nature. For human spiritual growth (good food), our Creator gives us directives with directions for us to learn and follow so we may coexist in harmony with all nature and each other, however, knowing there will never be a state of utopia. Both environments operate on a many-to-one ratio, as shown by the food chain providing energy on planet Earth within the scales of process and the order of magnitude and motion. When things get out of balance, undesirable results occur. For just one example, the gases that we inhale. Too much carbon monoxide will kill us. How much is too much? Less than a thousand parts per million. Less than one-hundredth of 1 percent. Not much at all.

THE NATURE OF GOD AND CREATION

First, my analysis shows that human desires for answers about creation are not a need but only a want and a nice-to-know since we can do nothing to change whatever has actually taken place. Some primitive pagan religions teach that the heavens, earth, and all living things, including humans, were created by God in six days about five thousand years ago, then Adam and Eve. One of the leading scientific theories is that of the big bang, which is kind of misleading, as it is more of a rapidly changing tiny point of matter. Perhaps they are both partially correct. Maybe that tiny point of matter rapidly changed because God's energy touched it. But not in six days. Then there is the age-old question: Which came first, the chicken or the egg? The only fact that I can find is that the egg is chicken, like a fetus is human.

Nonetheless, our Creator is the God of life and love, the highest form of pure energy that initially began motion in the heavens/space. Without motion, there would be no change, and time would not exist, only space as we perceive it to be. The process of nature is the designed methodology of our Creator so that biological life may exist and evolve. The process of nature has its own universal cycles of time. The cycles of time define which scale of process the change occurs based on the order of magnitude of the environment and the dimensions of time within the formation of all matter. According to science, all solid matter consists of various combinations of hydrogen and helium molecules, which are defined in the periodic table of known chemical elements, organized on the basis of their atomic number, weight, electron configurations, and with recurring chemical properties. They are the building blocks of life, matter formations, and the intended creations of our Creator using the natural processes and laws of nature.

In order for there to be molecular motion, heat/energy must be applied to stimulate activity. Heat can be generated from different sources: pressure, friction, chemical, or electrical. Yet all four require motion. In quantum physics, matter is the parts of parts. For every action, there is one or a series of cascading reactions both in the short and long term. The ramifications of one action can either be positive or negative, dependent upon the outcome of a singular motion.

This pertains to both physical and spiritual development. In the order of magnitude, for nature to work in the scales of process, there must be a flexible balance with constraints in the framework to stabilize the environment so biological life cycles may occur. All connected energy is in motion simultaneously in its own space. In the beginning of existence, it was our Creator's energy/heat that began the first natural motion of molecular change, including gravity, which they are still studying, the unseen energy we are all familiar with. From that point on, every reaction/motion was a natural chain reaction free to change and evolve over time in cycles within the blueprints of our Creator.

Our Creator does not interfere with the physical properties of natural motions directed by the laws of nature and the natural evolution of change. Metaphorically, though, nature's ways are the hands of our Creator, or the tools for the process of creation and existence. If anything changes in the physical universe, it is nature's way, not by way of our Creator directly. Our Creator does not use magic or miracles to alter physical matter. Physical change occurs from the perpetual motion of energy. While on the other hand, spiritual/nonvisible energy bands are also in perpetual motion where our Creator (positive) and the Destroyer (negative—evildoers) energies exist. Waves of energies in continuous motion, each within the scales of process defined by the order of its magnitude in relation to the cycles of vibrations. Something similar is taught in Hinduism. The waves just keep coming.

By the universal laws of nature, both the positive and negative energies use their energy to try to influence the conscience and sub-conscience human thought process. Each mind is programmed differently by their environment and life cycle experiences, establishing their own initial reactions to any situation based on their emotional primal feelings and its free will, good or bad as it may be.

Every other living species other than the human being is directly controlled by their natural, primal instinct for survival—from a simplex, single cell to a complex, multiplex cell structure (from a virus to a whale)—free to live and grow as they may in their own environment. Nature's biological energy management system is a balanced food chain and water. Our ancestors evolved over the millenniums to be free as all the other creatures surviving by primal instinct. From the Ramapithecus (over twelve million years ago) to the Homo habilis (around six million years ago, with at least two known cousins, the Africanus and Boisei species, going extinct), leaving the Homo erectus with a brain of conscious thought and a free will (around a million years ago).

As Homo erectus left Africa, learning what they could eat, changing their diet, so changed their physical bodies, bringing about the Homo sapiens and Homo sapiens neanderthalensis (around 150 thousand years ago). Plus, nine or more other humanoid sub-species until around seventy-four thousand years ago when the super volcano, Mount Toba, erupted, with only the Homo sapiens and Homo sapiens neanderthalensis surviving in the aftermath. About forty thousand years ago, the Neanderthals became extinct, leaving only the Homo sapiens as the dominant species. The anthropologists are not sure of the reason for the extinction of the Neanderthals. My analysis suggests that they went extinct because they trusted the Homo sapiens. They were the only others around at the time. Up to that point of natural evolution, our ancestors only needed water, food, shelter, security, and sanitation for survival. They were guided by their primal instinct, only needing clothing later in colder climates as they migrated, driven by the available food supplies as the population expanded with primitive tools being used.

This period marked a major milestone in the natural process of human evolution and mutations required for our Creator to be able to plant spiritual seeds, which we call our souls. As our physical bodies reflect the foods we eat, physically, we become what we eat. Spiritually, our individual minds need food to grow, fed to our heads, in order for our souls to grow and be harvested at the end of our life cycle. Having free will to discard the bad food (poison) and keep the good food (healthy) as our minds and souls (spiritual energy) also become what we keep inside. Soon after humans had the gift of reason and thought, some began to wonder about life, who created us, and why we are here, generating the emotion of fear of the unknown.

Cultures began creating various gods brought about by superstitions for an answer to those questions. Whatever the stories were, people bought into them just to make themselves feel comfortable. The first step of human spiritual evolution is being consciously aware of a higher power. Some very primitive cultures even engaged in human sacrifice to their gods. While others just one step ahead of them would sacrifice animals to their gods instead of people. The next step for human spiritual evolution was the creation of religious cults.

The leaders gave themselves the position of authority over the others, making a power grab as the Romans with the civilized teachings of Jesus. Some realized that they could use religion for power and control of their societies and in the local communities, abusing the ignorant masses with false claims embedded within their doctrines of civilized, common sense, human behavior. The wolves were hiding in sheep's clothing, killing and fighting each other over false teachings about our Creator. Millions of innocent people have been killed over their religious hate of each other, continuing to do so because they believe the lies of the false teachers and preachers who will never admit the truth about the true nature of God, our Creator. Most don't even know what they do while others try to capitalize.

In the scales of human process, humanity was just like a newborn baby without a spiritual user's manual. Previously, people's desires were only concerned with what they needed to survive. With free will, people began to have wants, and that started a conflict of interest between the nature of our

Creator and human nature. Each culture had different ideas about the unseen energies of creation driven by pagan superstitions, creating various ideologies, many gods, and fears of the unknown. Humanity as a whole is on the path of learning how to grow up and be civilized by conforming to the laws of our Creator and the laws of nature.

Technically, all biological life-forms are parasites, needing a living host (Mother Earth) to live off a many-to-one food chain, the natural scales of process. It is against the laws of nature for a parasite to kill its host. Even a new microscopic virus will learn and mutate so that it does not kill off its natural environmental host while the host works on building up a natural immunity to the new organism. Though throughout the scales of process, there are radical transgressors that do not adhere to the physical laws of nature, such as malignant cancer cells and some other parasites. This also holds true in the dimension of natural spiritual energies—some positive, some negative.

Humanity is aware of the responsibility placed on our shoulders to maintain a healthy living environment, protecting our host and the other creatures on our home planet, painfully trying to make adjustments in order to maintain a healthy environment for all life on Earth, counterbalancing humanity's use and tendencies of abuse (greed) of our natural resources and each other.

Depending on one's predefined destiny in life, some have more than they need while others struggle to survive. For those struggling to survive, it is up to the individual's free will and free choice to improve their living conditions if they are willing. God helps those who try and help themselves by giving proper guidance when asking/praying for proper guidance by thoughts received or even in dreams. Unfortunately, as mentioned previously, the negative energies use the same process to influence our thoughts to ignore God's guidance and take what may look like an easier solution, as is human nature by the majority, like water running down a mountainside will take the path of least resistance. Humans were created by God using nature as the process. To address human behaviors, cultures use fear and the threat of repercussions for breaking civilized laws, which still is the approach for controlling the masses within their defined jurisdictions.

With the two major religions of Christianity and Islam, Satan has you right where evil wants you, putting your faith and believing in false perceptions of our Creator, willing to kill each other from hate of those who were taught to believe something else. This is the primary reason why people should not hold on to the ignorance of human racial or religious prejudice, bias, and hatred. To go through life carrying these two types of hatred in your mind only generates negative energy and weight to one's soul and prevents peace from one's life. Human racial and religious prejudice followed by hatred are taught, not natural.

Religions are of human creation, defining God in their image, as our Creator does not have a physical body, with some leaders who want to abuse their authority for control over their flocks and feed their egos. A diversity of thought, though, in an attempt to accomplish the same fundamental objectives in an effort to create and maintain order based upon their demographic cultures, customs, and charity.

People who are taught to be racial and/or religious prejudiced have been programmed with mental malware. We all have forms of mental malware with varying degrees, as none of us are perfect, from the garbage we keep in our heads. Part of the cost of having a free will to choose and freedom to move about is about having to learn how to be a responsible person and being held accountable for uncivilized behavior. One way or the other, we sleep in the bed we make. Some call it karma. Human spiritual evolution starts with people being honest with themselves and about the true realities of life, like adhering to the guidelines of the jurisdictional authorities.

Jurisdictional authority is multidimensional, with our Creator's jurisdictional authority at the top. The first dimension is directives/laws for the formation of all matter. The second-dimension directives pertain to the creation of biological life, with natural instinct preprogrammed for survival, like how unborn infants suck their thumbs to exercise the muscles that will be needed for their first meal after birth. Thirdly are the directions for human nature and behavior. Fourth are laws defined by humans (civil and criminal codes). Fifth are family rules defined by the parents and guardians of the young.

Being that humans have a free will tied to primal instinct, God had to define a separate list of directions for us to follow for the evolution of civilized behavior, knowing some will comply and others will not by individual free choice. Learning God's directions starts at the bottom, with the parents or guardians teaching a young child the difference between proper and improper civilized behavior (transgressions). Then comes the religious indoctrination, depending on the parents' choice of theology. As with the scales of process, there are the scales of transgressions connected to the order of magnitude and the weight of the negative results, current and residual. Transgressions occur in both the physical and spiritual dimensions.

Within each society, various civil codes are enacted, defining what they perceive as civilized behavior and the ramifications of uncivilized behavior. Within the societies, there are various cultures defined by the religious cults addressing the spiritual dimension. Each cult has its own perception of the spiritual world of existence, aware of the energy of our Creator yet blinded by what they cannot see, even killing others who will not conform to their cult, creating biases and hatred toward others, generating transgressions in their herds. This is the exact opposite of what our God of creation desires from us and is preventing human spiritual evolution from occurring. Though for the most part, the religious cults understand and teach the moral principles of civilized behaviors.

Within the various cultures, sports and games are a way of teaching about rules and regulations to children, with penalties for breaking the rules or stepping out of bounds, which is also a very positive, civilized way to bring people together. Yet, like religions, there are the fanatics who spoil it for the rest from time to time—like parents getting too serious at sporting events, sometimes physically assaulting the officials in front of all the children. Every now and then, we hear about adults going crazy at soccer matches, causing people to die. Somehow, I don't think that any of those people who have died from going to watch a game thought that they would meet their fate, their destiny, that day.

Upon physical death, our soul's spiritual energy is released to the spiritual dimension of our Creator's domain, dust to dust, our bodies remain. God does not judge us by our transgressions; that is not how our souls and our spiritual energy reunite with God's energy. It is by our free will to follow the directions (spiritual user manual) of our Creator and nature during our individual, temporary life cycle. Thus, showing our gratefulness, gratitude, worship, and our love for our Creator. It is the weight of negative energy in our minds and souls that pollutes our souls through the things we choose to do, stopping a soul from reconnecting with too much extra baggage. Our souls, like other vessels, have a capacity, holding only so much energy until it runs out and over. Some positive and some negative. To get rid of the residual negative energies of one's past, first, one must stop generating more by their actions. Then by helping others and doing good deeds, generating more positive energy and pushing out the negative energies. Frankly, I have no idea as to what the weight limits are.

The numbers of nature—many acorns and few trees. Many sperm cells (a million plus), and one—sometimes a few more lucky egg hunters—is born, but only a few are born out of the multitude. Many people, but only a few souls return. Not by God's choice but by individual free will to choose how to live their spiritual and physical life. Worship is not about going to a church; the only way to worship God is by adhering to the few directions for civilized behavior and individual spiritual development.

The laws of physical nature to exist are many and very complex, all linked together like the fibers of a piece of string, the parts of parts. There are various fields of study, from astrophysics to microbiology, learning about the laws of nature. Just as there are many theologies trying to learn and understand the directives and directions of God's spiritual nature that actually are few, so they are not hard to learn or remember and are easy to understand, defined by positive behaviors and negative transgressions, addressing individual actions, emotions, and thoughts that must be avoided to keep the robes of our minds and souls as clean as humanly possible.

THE CRITICAL DO'S AND DON'TS FOR INDIVIDUAL SPIRITUAL EVOLUTION

The do's

1. Love and respect our Creator, our host planet, and all life.
2. Procreate, survive, evolve naturally, and learn to be civilized.
3. Teach your children well for the sake of their souls, yours, and the rest of us.

The don'ts

1. *Do not kill* except for food or in self-defense.
2. *Do no harm* to others except in self-defense.
3. *Do not steal.*
4. *Do not misspeak.*
5. *Do not abuse.*

PROCESS REVIEW FOR INDIVIDUAL SPIRITUAL EVOLUTION

The do's

1. *Love and respect our Creator, our host planet, and all life.*

    Our Creator's natural spiritual directions define the positive moral values of behavior so that the human race may evolve and become a truly civilized species over time, providing the proper food for our spiritual development in order to increase the harvesting of our souls. Nature's directives address the physical life. All living species have the freedom to multiply and live as Mother Nature evolves, without any bias. Our Creator's conscience existence living energy is not of physical matter and void of our physical desires motivated or manipulated by our emotions, desires that compel some people to make bad decisions during their cycle of life, slowly putting the weight of negative energies on their souls at the expense of other's rights of life and freedoms.

Physical life in the universe is scarce and precious, a gift of our Creator. Our souls are the seeds of our Creator, the spiritual energy in each of us that makes us equal at birth, pure and uncontaminated. God loves us as a parent loves their children.

In return, our Creator wants us to show our love, respect, and appreciation by living within the natural guidelines of civilized behavior and by taking care of all that God, through physical and spiritual nature, has created. This includes, for those who can, helping out others in temporary need and pointing them in the right direction for any long-term solutions then sending them on their way. Help the children as much as possible. If you need a ritual to worship our Creator, be it an act of help and kindness to others when the opportunity occurs. One person's problems are not the responsibility of others, but helping those in need is a positive action in motion. Help and support is not *enabling* someone to continue their self-destructive behaviors.

2.   *Procreate, survive, evolve naturally, and learn to become civilized.*

Procreation creates a conflict of interest between nature and human behaviors. For all the other living species, including plant life, nature's cycles send signals when it is time for them to propagate. Humans, on the other hand, with free will, would not copulate unless it was a pleasurable process. Some people are confused with the emotional and spiritual feelings of love and physical feelings of sexual lust. People are free to love whomever they will emotionally, but that doesn't mean they should engage in same-sex physical lust. That is the opposite of civilized human behavior. The vast majority of people seek feelings of physical and mental comfort, pleasure, and immediate self-gratification, which is human and animal nature actually. In the process of copulation, the immediate self-gratification feeling of pleasure peaks out at the point of climax as a personal reward for following the directives of nature to propagate and produce a baby. Nature's true intent of our reproductive organs is to be used between a male and a female *only*.

What determines a person's physical gender during development are what we call X and Y genes. A female is born with an XX set of genes while a male is born with an XY set of genes. Unseen physical gender abnormalities occur when there is an imbalance between the parents' gene pool. Any physical part of our reproductive systems can and occasionally get out of balance, causing physical deformities—physically so much so some unfortunate people are born with a scrotum and a vagina, the only true human hermaphrodites. The numbers are about the same as that for a mother giving birth to a set of Siamese twins.

The human procreation process has five natural stages.

Stage 1: from birth through prepuberty.

Stage 2: puberty and the development of our reproductive organs.

Stage 3: the physical ability to procreate.

Stage 4: menopause that shuts down the ability to reproduce.

Stage 5: postmenopause.

Boys experience different changes than girls, and all children have their own time periods of development. The time frames for both sexes vary slightly, as females (girls) can begin to experience the physical changes anywhere from eight years old to fourteen years of age and normally finish their cycle of puberty by sixteen. While males (boys) can begin to experience their changes around nine years old up to fourteen, yet the normal age is around eleven.

When issues out of the norm occur, it is more than likely an imbalance caused by issues with hormones and or glands. The changes in physical development also impact the mental state of being for a child going through puberty, bringing about various degrees of individual reactions and emotional mood shifts, both in the puberty and menopause stages.

By the time a child reaches puberty, most understand the reality that only a woman can give birth to a baby, as only a woman has ovaries that produces the eggs. While only a male can produce the seeds, a human reality of nature. By the time a child reaches the age of five, they know from observation that only a real woman can give birth to a baby. Yet they do not know how a woman becomes pregnant unless they observe animals copulating and someone explains it to them. Procreation comes under the jurisdictional authority of the laws of nature. The prime example of the need for law and order to define the guidelines of behavior and reactions of motion. From matter solidifying, chemical responses, biological cellular development, the food chain, and the human spiritual development—all require fundamental principles to work as one complex, cohesive unit to maintain order and balance.

Nature is perfect when proper balance is maintained within operational boundaries. Because of the vastness of the universe, occasionally, things get slightly out of balance here and there physically and spiritually. Physically, when any creature experiences a state of unbalanced development, physical deformities occur unintended—such as missing a limb, weak organs, blindness, deafness, brain formation, or any part of the structure.

Spiritually, during the development of the human individual consciousness, things also get out of balance, causing issues in personal decisions and behaviors as a result of unbalanced physical brain formation or information / bad data given to a person's mind after birth. Yet the subconscious mind is controlled by primal instinct and the laws of nature to survive. In the Information Age, like a computer BIOS, what is really amazing about nature's directives of survival is that when our bodies are invaded by bacterial or viral cells, our body's natural response is to create antibodies for natural immunity starting after we are first born or by our parents' genetics—something beyond our physical control. In the process, mammal's bodies are programmed to generate a fever to kill off the invader. And if you scientists seem to think that it is just a coincidence of nature, think again. That takes us to learning how to become civilized.

3. *Teach your children.*

Our Creator's intentions are for people to have a free choice for a mate (natural selection) of the opposite sex with whom they choose to have as a lifetime partner out of mutual love, respect, and trust. Marry, produce children, and raise a family. It is the parents' responsibility to raise their children with a proper education and mindset of civilized, moral behaviors so that the children will grow up to become an asset and not be a liability to themselves, their family, community, and their country. Through the cycles of life, the individual physical and spiritual development depends on the food that is fed to the body and the head. A young child's mind is the most fragile thing in the universe. Yet it is humanity's greatest resource. Be careful of what you put inside.

The don'ts

1.   *Do not kill except for food or in self-defense.*
     Every living creature on our planet—from the microscopic insects, body mites crawling on your skin (parasites), to the elephants and whales in the water—is all under the control of the laws of primal nature,

instinct to maintain a balance of nature, except for our species. Not only is this a law of nature but it is also a law at every level of human jurisdictional authority (sadly, depending on where one lives), yet showing advancement/evolving toward becoming a civilized species.

Human nature requires for those with lesser intelligence (who don't value their freedoms of life or others) that there be harsh punishments (death to life imprisonment) to dissuade them from misusing their free will to steal a life that is not theirs to take. Hate is the heaviest spiritual transgression, and killing is the heaviest physical transgression. Both transgressions / personal actions carry a heavy cost on our minds and souls.

2.   *Do no harm to others except in self-defense.*
No one should or has the right to assault another person, inflicting bodily inju-

ries or engaging in activities that negatively impact other people's lives. Victims of those impacted by other people's transgressions do have a right to self-defense, and other civilized people have a duty to come to the aid of someone in need of help if they are able. Do not force others against their free will.

All organized societies have established laws and codes of punishment depending on the magnitude of the infraction in an effort for it to become a more civilized society. This does not mean that all laws are fair and just, and proper discretion needs to be used in the application of law and order. The codes of punishment deal with human nature as a deterrent in an effort to maintain order within the levels of the jurisdictional authorities. Whereas, most people will understand that the crime is not worth the lost time and the loss of their freedoms. Nor do they have a criminal mentality.

Why do human societies break down over a period of time? There is a law of physical and mental (human) nature that dictates, if something is going to break, it will break at the weakest point from pressure. In societies, the weakest point can be found to be the mindset of the people weakened by a slow deterioration of the moral values that define a civilized society. From an individual to a nation, when falling on hard times, they will do things that they normally would not do, trying to survive. Evil energy (the devil?) will attack at the weakest point and try to manipulate the thoughts and actions of those involved, only compounding the problems, using the situation to falsely justify their choice of options (physical actions) for relief.

For human societies, there is a process cycle of war, learning, and forgetting. War, learn, and forget… After a few generations, the lessons learned from the last conflicts are forgotten. The quality of leadership declines, and chaos eventually erupts. Since the first Sumerian society over fifty-five hundred years ago learned to write, to this day and age, when life becomes better than it had been, people become complacent, and ill-minded people take control of the society's business process management regardless of the form of government. Today, around the globe, moral values have been replaced with money. Do no harm encompasses many things. Doing harm to others is a choice made and puts more dirt on people's robes that are there to protect the souls of people and that of society.

3.   *Do not steal.*

Do not steal sounds straightforward. Yet it encompasses more than just money or material goods, which accounts for the majority of transgressions. For example, slavery forces others to relinquish their natural God-given right to freedom in order for someone else to profit from their labor and time. This has been going on since the beginning of human societies and still to this day. Now there are more people being forced into having sex than other types of slavery even in countries claiming to be civilized societies.

Killing is also a form of stealing, taking the life of another person whose life doesn't belong to them. Some also steal the life from the dead person's family. The four main reasons are hatred, money, sex, or being jealous of another person. Then there are some who will have sex with someone else's spouse, causing a divorce. If children are involved, then stealing from them in their family unit.

Lesser transgressions are things like intentionally wasting other people's time or attempting to convince someone to give their time, energy, money, or something they have of personal value, misrepresenting their intentions, even if they are not successful. Being jealous of what others have is a negative personal feeling, also magnified when trying to take or steal whatever it is one is jealous of. Yet over time, the weight of lesser transgressions adds up.

From the individual to nations with bad leadership, people engage in such uncivilized behavior. With human nature, stealing is a choice of free will, like taxation without representation. Now, with technology, stealing is running rampant around the globe. People don't even have to leave their homes to steal from someone else anywhere around the globe in just a matter of minutes, and law enforcement is overwhelmed. The best policy is, if it is not yours, leave it alone. Don't touch it! If you need or want something, earn or make it.

Who loses the most when someone steals something from someone else? The person who was stolen from or the thief who has already lost their self-dignity, respect, honor, and the trust of others, or they wouldn't do what they do. That will depend on what one values. Some people will still be friends and associates of a thief, but they know better than to trust them. As they will know that if their friend is a thief, the friend will steal from them should the opportunity present itself.

4. *Do not misspeak.*

Technically, when someone says or writes something that is not true or correct and is not a factual reality, they tell a lie, fabricating a false reality. A factual reality is that there are two realities here; one deals with facts, the other fiction. In the Bible, one of their commandments states, "Thou shall not bear false witness against thy neighbor." It addresses only one type of transgression in relation to what people lie about when a truer statement would be, "Thou shall not bear false witness against anyone."

A human reality is that some people just don't care about misspeaking and are clueless about moral values and of their personal integrity. There are far too many reasons why people lie about things to itemize the transgression of misspeaking. In general, the bad types of lies are because people are in the process or have done something that they know is not right in a civilized society. People in our governments and religions have been misspeaking for a few thousand years to control the minds of other people. Another quirk of human nature is that we pay for the mistakes of our ancestors by not learning from theirs and our own mistakes.

There are good lies, and we call these stories fiction. Cultures have used fictional stories to teach their children about the principles of civilized, moral behaviors. So long as those who speak or write make it clear that it is fictional, no transgression has occurred. Before humans could write, the only way to teach about their culture's history was by word of mouth over the centuries. Some people who have retold the history stories have made their own edits, exaggerating to make the story a little bit better, slightly making changes over time. These stories are called fables, which contain some truth with some fiction, going all the way back to Moses and their Ten Commandments. Here is a secret they don't want people to understand. God did not give Moses commandments to obey. God gave Moses directions, like a treasure map to follow, so that our souls would be able to get back home. The right approach, like God, helped me to see the true reality of human existence. Yet I had to figure out the words to write, as had Moses. The part about the burning bush was so Moses could claim that the directions came directly from God. If Moses took ownership, people could argue with him. By saying the words came from God, he knew people could not argue with him about the directions. People can argue with others and themselves, but one thing we can't do is argue with God. God blessed me with self-evident truths to write, and whether or not you believe me is not of my concern.

Regardless, when people get caught lying about serious issues, they are the biggest loser, like getting caught stealing. They lose the trust of those who know them. People, in general, do not really like people whom they cannot trust. People sometimes mistakenly misspeak, and those with personal integrity will apologize and admit to their error. This normally occurs because they were given bad data by someone whom they trusted and did not verify what information they received.

True leadership uses the truth to motivate people to do the right things. While false leaders (evildoers) use lies and deceptions to manipulate people to do things they should not do. The weight of the transgression of misspeaking on a person's soul depends on how many people are negatively impacted by the lie and whether or not it was intentionally spoken.

5.   *Do not abuse or misuse.*
The process of abusing anything is simply a matter of someone's free will and is never necessary, only a choice. Abuse is the misuse of power, both physically and mentally, caused by negative energies. Human nature dictates that if there is anything to be abused, someone or more than one person will find a way to abuse whatever it is. In this time period, humans have created automobiles, and people die every day from abusing travel

speed. We have developed aircraft, and some have intentionally flown them into high-rise office buildings filled with people. Our new technology, the Internet, is something else the evildoers abuse, evolving to using artificial intelligence, making it even easier for some to abuse.

Since the development of our species, people have abused each other. As we evolved into tribal cultures, which marks the beginning of humanity's effort to become a civilized species, people in charge have misused, used, and abused their authority. Control was and still is maintained by the abilities of physical force. Whether it be a single person, tribe, clan, gang, or at the national level, people continue to abuse each other. Our advancements in the field of medicine are absolutely remarkable. There is a group of doctors called Doctors Without Borders doing good and helping people. Then there is a group of Doctors Without Souls, who are sexually mutilating the bodies of children because they can for a profit. Since the creation of currency, people find ways of abusing money, which is used as a weapon to control other people.

Initially, rules of behavior and punishment were defined by tribal customs and traditions to deal with those who would not comply with what was viewed as honorable and civil behavior by a member of their tribe. Today there are the scums of scribes that abuse the applications of laws and their jurisdictional authority because they can, holding justice up for ransom if you can afford their fees.

Human sexual abuses—the conflict here is that some people will misuse and abuse their reproductive organs to artificially induce a false sense of physical pleasure in climaxing with no intent of producing and raising a child, only engaging in sex parties. In various societies, primarily in the Western world, too many people are very confused about the reality of nature's process of procreation. So this subject matter needs review to help clarify the reality of nature. The intent of our Creator is for a man and a woman to freely choose their spouse, procreate, and raise and teach their children how to be civilized until adulthood. It is the parents' or guardians' responsibility and right to raise children to become a responsible, civilized human being.

The vast majority of parents do try to teach and to train their children on the moral principles of civilized behavior. This includes the reality that copulating may produce another human life, and most people understand this fact. Yet whether being a child or an adult, people still freely engage in irresponsible, unprotected sexual activities. Not only this but some very misguided, mentally ill people engage in same-sex sexual activities to falsely induce the feelings of procreation.

Just as there are a good number of negative physical possibilities occurring with our reproductive organs, there are also a good number of negative mental possibilities that can occur during some people's lives so much so they are in complete denial of what their natural sex is, suffering from PTSD. They refuse to comply with the laws of nature, thinking that they are something that they are not. The real problem is not what is between their legs. The real problem is what is in their minds between their ears.

For a good majority of these victims, what got put in their minds happened at an early age by someone older already suffering from being molested and PTSD. Another critical point is that whatever may have happened as a young child is that they don't consciously remember the transgression, or for self-protection, their minds blocked out the physical transgressions. It is clearly a mental delusional reaction to rejecting reality. The chains of evil continue to grow through the passage of time. Then there are those who become addicted to engaging in sexual activities—a process of self-medicating, like some people do with substance abuse, including food, using physical and mental pleasure to temporarily escape the realities of their lives and generating a false sense of well-being.

It is said that prostitution is the oldest profession. Why? Because that was the only thing some women had to sell to survive. It did not make them evil; they were only out of options. Yet they were using a man's primal instinct to propagate, marketing and feeding their desires. For a few thousand years, there have been those who have enslaved women and children, creating a sex-slave industry

still in operation and growing. Media com-
mercials are saturated with sexual content,
using sex to sell their products, a form of sexual predatorial behavior taking advantage of
human primal instincts, as one religion uses
for false promises to the males after death.
Interestingly enough, just last week, the
other one just started to let their priest bless
same-sex marriages, starving for more sheeple. Yeah, well, the oldest con job is selling
religion. One of the biggest lies being told is
that God made man in his own image. The
reality there is that man/men made a false
image of our Creator for their purposes.

In some parts of the world, there are
people using sexual perversion as a political
weapon against the children in their schools,
trying to remove any sense of civilized and
moral behavior, calling themselves educators.
Then there are those whose minds have been
twisted that engage in same-gender sex and

same-gender marriage, misusing and abusing their reproductive organs for a temporary sense of personal pleasure driven by sexual lust. Some people are even worse, those who molest children or force someone else to engage in unwanted sexual activities. All these people are evildoers under demonic control, lacking self-control as those also who enable and support them. Evil garbage has been injected into their minds.

Male or female, married or not, young or old, when people see members of the opposite sex that stimulate their primal instinct, thoughts of physical desires will surface, and that is a natural reaction. Being physically attracted to the same sex is not a natural reaction nor is it nature's intention. It is a reaction of those suffering from severe mental issues or born with mental handicaps and should be treated as such.

When someone tells these poor people the truth of the matter, the speakers of the truth are called names like homophobe, transphobe, and other such names because they have no solid ground to stand on. When in reality, they fear what sex nature made them and refuse to acknowledge or accept the truth. They claim that the people who oppose their sexual perversions are using hate speech when the majority of those who do oppose their uncivilized behaviors actually pity them. What most people hate is the evil, uncivilized garbage they are feeding to other people's children's minds and contaminating their souls, stealing a child's innocence. Why? Because someone has stolen theirs.

A woman has the right to choose with whom they want to engage with in their sex parties. The cost of this right to choose is about being personally responsible for their reproductive organs. When they are irresponsible and become pregnant from having a sex party, that does not give them the personal right to kill their unborn child or to make others pay for their abortions to clean up their messes after their sex parties. There is absolutely no way to stop people from having sex. That's not going to happen. A reality, though, is that *only you can prevent an abortion*. If a woman has an abortion, then her tubes should be tied, as well as the male involved, to prevent repeated transgressions. Law of human nature: two wrongs don't make it right. In the scales of the process, guys need to become more like the pot growers. Be very careful of where you plant your seeds! I know, easier said than done. I was once young. There's a lot of things that I don't know, and one of them is how much is having too much sex. I don't have a clue.

With the explosion of the mass media, the Internet, and corporations pushing sex to sell their goods, most today have a good idea about human sexual activities and how a woman gets pregnant. The issue here is, again, part of the human nature of children wanting to do what they see the adults are doing: drinking, doing other drugs, and sexual pleasures. Monkey see, monkey do. If a child has been given a proper moral understanding of the reality and consequences of engaging in unmarried sexual activities, then a parent has done the best that they could do.

The reality here is such that some kids don't always listen to their parents and teachers. Right? Then there are a lot of people who should not be teaching children or even having children as far as that goes. These are the people who do not want to comply with the directions of responsible, civilized, moral values; the ones who do not care about things like personal integrity or the meaning of personal and family honor; the ones who make children pay for their ignorance, putting garbage in their heads. This is another approach of evil using the human reproductive system as a weapon against the efforts by some to become a civilized, God-respecting species.

Those who pass laws against the laws of nature and creation have the blood of those unborn children on their hands and souls as much as the woman who has an abortion. Killing an unborn child is about as uncivilized as cannibalism. Natural common sense dictates that just because one can do something does not mean that one should or has a right to do so. Another, too much of a good thing is never a good thing, including abusing our reproductive organs. For some men, having too much sex may cause their prostate glands to become enlarged and have residual health issues later in life. Oh, before I forget again, there are all the sexually transmitted diseases (STDs) to look out for.

People need to become more conscientiously aware of and understand what is taking place with nature's prime directive to propagate, and learn to use proper discretion with the use of their reproductive organs. Learn to let those thoughts go and not act upon hormonal impulses. Unless they are in the market for a mate of the opposite sex to start a family. Another one of those easier-said-than-done things.

Billions of dollars are spent annually around the globe by people buying products to try and make themselves look attractive and sexy—mostly by females even after they are married. That's not even counting the money spent on media advertisement.

Sexual perversions against nature's intent and laws that contaminate one's mind and soul, the transgressions' weight varies, like same-gender sex, molesting a child, rape, choosing an abortion because of not being a responsible person, misusing your reproductive organs, or other uncivilized sexual activities, will prevent a soul's energy from reunification with our Creator's energy upon one's death. Perhaps the lesser of sexual transgressions is masturbation, depending on what one is fantasizing about. It is not going to cause an abortion and should not get any STDs.

The next step is understanding why we do the things we do. For the most part, what we do is a response to our emotional state of mind. Emotions are a primal instinct as can be observed and verified by watching other creatures—from the insects, reptiles, aquatic life, other mammals, and humans. All living creatures besides humans have a built-in, nat-ural, immediate-response survival mechanism triggering their initial emotional impulse and reaction to a given situation, next generating a thought, a decision process to determine what to do or say next. Creatures in the wild even have choices—flee, fight, freeze, feed, or fornicate—depending. They do have limited options and have to make decisions. What is so amazing about the nature of our Creators is that every living creature, micro to mammoth, is a power-generating plant of operation within the natural scales of process, each with their own anatomy and metabolism. Simply by the vast number of living species on our planet, it is clear that life is not just a coincidence of nature's creations. What else is amazing about our physical designs and the emotion of fear is that as soon as the emotion is felt, our bodies release adrenaline, which turbocharge our physical response. Coincidence? No.

Nature tells a bird to build a nest, but it is up to the bird to find a safe place to build the nest. If you have ever been stung by a bee or bit by an insect or animal, it is because it was upset and felt threatened. On the other hand, depending on the type of bee, most bees are the happiest with their face in a flower. For those of you who have had pets for a long time, you can see their emotional response and even attitudes. Immediate gratification is a natural desire, not just a human goal. When creatures get thirsty, they go to water. If hungry, they go hunting. If during the mating season or when in heat, they want to propagate, and they want it NOW! For some, the loss of their pet can be every bit as emotionally painful as losing a human loved one. For some dog owners, they provide a sense of emotional security and peace of mind.

Creatures in nature are territorial also. The desire to have a marked area for security is not just a human trait. Insects and animals will fight to protect their homes, offspring, and space—a law of nature. In the scales of the process, it is a leader's duty and responsibility to protect the people and the boundaries of their country. Anything less is a transgression against the laws of nature. Anything less is an act of treason. Why? Because they can, and it's their choice to choose money over morals to satisfy their emotions and desires. Human emotions generate thoughts, and thoughts feed our emotions, creating our personal desires for survival, pleasure, and a sense of well-being (egos).

Human thoughts can be generated from many sources. Thoughts can come from what we see, hear, smell, taste, and physically and mentally feel. One thought can create many thoughts. Thoughts create electrical pulses/internal waves of energy in our brains. Some thoughts are generated when we injure ourselves, and signals are processed through our central nervous system to our cerebral cortex (brains). The response scale can be from an ouch to a scream or strong enough to cause a person to go into shock, pass out, or cause a heart attack and die for some.

Just in the last two hundred years, people first learned to use wire for transmissions of energy signals. That led to the discovery and creativity of how to use radio waves, unseen energy bands, for transmission. Most of us have used or heard AM and FM broadcast on the radio. Just two bands are defined by the amount of energy used for transmissions, each bandwidth having the ability to simultaneously process multiple signals with a slight frequency variation. Now we have our cell phones using microwaves. What is interesting about radio waves is that they have physical characteristics demonstrated by the effects of the sun's energy during the daytime, creating resistance and interference in the transmissions. When facing away from the sun during nighttime, the atmosphere allows the signals to travel farther, which is the reason that here in the USA, the Federal Communications Commission (FCC) has them reduce the wattage output.

The first point of this is for awareness of the existence of the unseen spiritual energy bands, both good and evil, that can send signals of thoughts to our brains, generating other thoughts. Basically, the same way other people hack into our computers. In the scales of process, remote hacking is not a new concept. When thoughts come, which are detrimental to civilized individual behaviors, the negative energies are trying to manipulate us to do something that we shouldn't do. This occurs quite often when we are in a conflict of emotional stress, and at our weakest moments, wrong thoughts can emerge. That is when it is time for people who believe in God to change their thoughts into prayers for guidance. Even after people choose the wrong options, God will give thoughts of doubts about what you are in the process of doing wrong—too many times ignored. When you find yourself trying to justify what you are doing, you already know that they really ought not to proceed but let the emotional pressure dictate their desires and thoughts. It is only natural to look for the easy way out. As one of my teachers taught, good things start with the right thoughts. (Ah, that was Buddha.)

The second point about mentioning the unseen physical effects of electrical energies is that when our soul's energy departs from our physical bodies after death, the weight of the remaining transgressions creates resistance and interferes with our soul's ability to reconnect to our Creator's frequency of vibrations, stuck on another bandwidth. Here on earth, when we feel good vibrations, they just make us feel better. Then something else pops up, and they are gone. When people realize that they have put their faith in the wrong things, they will have reached a turning point and have the freedom to reevaluate what they have been told. As one of our teachers taught, "The truth will set you free."

Faith only does someone well when put into reality, not in primitive, pagan, passed-down stories. Do prayers do any good? Yes, they do. Yet only when praying for the right things. Since God doesn't micromanage (pick and choose) or change physical matter other than through the process of nature, prayers for others to be healed are in nature's hands, not God's hands directly. Spiritually, a lot of us pray for those who have too much trash in their heads, doing things we know they shouldn't be doing to themselves or to others. These prayers do get answered, and God will try and help these people with the right thoughts. That doesn't mean, though, that the person needing guidance will choose the right things to do because of our free will. What these prayers of hope do, though, is show that the person saying the prayers are compassionate and trying to be a civilized person with thoughts of goodwill generated by the emotion of sorrow and feelings for others' well-being. Sometimes we are helpless to help, and all we have to give are feelings of goodwill in a prayer. Send more for humanity, please.

We put it in God's hands when it is already in nature's hands and one's destiny physically. People pray for a lot of things when the odds are fifty-fifty, a positive or negative outcome. Perhaps enough prayers of positive energy vibrations focused toward someone hurt or sick could help their healing properties. I'm not going to try and tell people what to pray for or not; that's your free choice. I do know, though, that prayers trying to communicate with God work when asking for proper guidance and in giving thanks to God for what we do have and all the other types of beautiful life on earth in a cold and desolate universe. When we show our appreciation by action, we receive more of whatever. God will provide us with options, but it is our free choice to choose between doing something or not. So it might appear that our prayers have gone unanswered, sometimes causing one to cry, like a parent whose child dies from an overdose.

SUMMARY

In conclusion, every person on our planet needs to understand the common realities about each other which are defined by the Corner-Stone and Foundation of Human Understanding. Demonstrated with the eight questions of self-evident truths, answered by you the reader. Truths that the religious fanatics will not want others to comprehend, trying to block the way of Human Spiritual Evolution for their own personal benefits and self-proclaimed positions of false authority. Yes, too many lost souls in this epic time period of human history in the year 2024.

One of our strongest emotions is that of fear and fear of the unknown. That is what created mythologies, gods, and religious cults. Each cult with its own theory as to who, what, when, and how existence came to be. That is why the study of religions is called Theology, theories and concepts to explain the reality of energies unseen. Then came those who learned to use cults as a way of controlling and unifying large groups of people, fabricating answers to people's superstitions.

The religions mix the good food of thoughts incurring civilized behaviors with their false perceptions of the supernatural domain of our Creator (with different names). Another quirk of human nature, if you keep repeating a lie, some people will begin to believe the lie or lies. Populations are indoctrinated and brainwashed from birth, and that is another light of truth. Again, religions are only a stepping stone in the evolution of human spirituality. That is unless we kill off our species over religion, greed, other's desire to control our planet, or an act of nature first.

The question of: Are there any other living planets with life out in the Universe besides Earth? The Natural Scales of Process says yes, more than likely. One to many and many to one. Plus, I don't think God puts all of the eggs in one basket. Yet, why would they want to interact with a warring Species still stuck in spiritual diapers?

Fortunately for us, what religious theology we were taught to believe in or not is irrelevant, and our Creator knows the reality of why people think and believe the things they do. What is relevant, though, is doing one's best to follow the directions of the civilized Do's and Don'ts. It's your life, your soul, and your free choice. Facts or fiction? May God guide and be with you always. AMEN!

The Last Messenger

9 7 9 8 8 9 3 1 5 2 7 4 6